NAVAJO

Visions and Voices Across the Mesa

▽   ▽   ▽

NAVAJO

Visions and Voices Across the Mesa

▽   ▽   ▽

SHONTO BEGAY

SCHOLASTIC
HARDCOVER

SCHOLASTIC INC.
New York

To my family,

for their love and patience: my wife, Cruz;

my daughters, Enei, Reina, and Shonri; and my son, Dante;

and to my father, Mailboy, and my mother, Faye,

for their stories and strength.

———————

Copyright © 1995 by Shonto Begay
All rights reserved
Published by Scholastic Inc.
SCHOLASTIC HARDCOVER
is a registered trademark of Scholastic Inc.

No part of this publication may be reproduced in whole
or in part, or stored in a retrieval system, or transmitted in any form or by
any means, electronic, mechanical, photocopying, recording, or otherwise, without
written permission of the publisher. For information regarding permission,
write to Scholastic Inc., 555 Broadway, New York, NY 10012.

Library of Congress Cataloging-in-Publication Data
Begay, Shonto.   Navajo: visions and voices across the mesa
Shonto Begay.   p.   cm.
ISBN 0-590-46153-2   1. Navajo Indians—Poetry.
I. Title.   PS3552.E3717V57
1995   811'.54—dc20   93-31610   CIP

12 11 10 9 8 7 6 5 4 3 2 1   5 6 7 8 9 0/0 9

Printed in Singapore   First printing, March 1995

The text type in this book was set in Aldus by WLCR New York, Inc.
Color separations were made by Bright Arts, Ltd., Singapore.
Printed and bound by Tien Wah Press, Singapore
Production supervision by Angela Biola
Design by Kathleen Westray

CONTENTS

▽　▽　▽

INTRODUCTION 6

Echoes 9

Creation 10

Mother's Lace 13

Grandmother 14

Reflections After the Rain 17

Darkness at Noon: *Solar Eclipse* 18

In My Mother's Kitchen 21

Many Faces, Many Stories 23

Second Night 25

Night Holds Mysteries 26

Death Hogan 28

Lifeline 31

Down Highway 163 33

Navajo Power Plant 34

Storm Pattern 37

Coyote Crossing 38

Our Mysteries, His Knowledge 40

Anasazi Diaspora 42

Into the New World 45

Early Spring 46

INDEX OF PAINTINGS 48

INTRODUCTION

▽　▽　▽

THE PAINTINGS AND POEMS in this book explore facets of Navajo life that are rarely touched upon in Western literature. They will take you into the corners of my world, the Navajo world, so that you may experience daily life on the mesa in the twentieth century. You will also feel the echoes and reverberations of the way things were here on the mesa many hundreds of years before Columbus.

Having grown up in this particular culture during the fifties and sixties, I felt a strong need to reconnect to the history of my people and to my own personal history, through art and poetry.

When I was five, I was sent to a government boarding school, where I stayed until my eighth-grade year. By law, Navajo children had to go. The government wanted to assimilate us as quickly as it could. We were not allowed to speak our own language. If we were caught speaking Navajo, our mouths were washed out with soap. We were also forced to go to government-sponsored churches. We were only permitted to go home for two weeks during Christmas, and for the summer. Our parents were forbidden from seeing us in between those times. It was believed that losing our culture would make us become successful.

When I was in the fifth grade, things suddenly changed. It was the 1960s. And with the social movements came a time of great happiness. We no longer were punished for speaking our own language. And we no longer had to go to foreign churches if we didn't want to. It was a time of great strength for us.

Many people still grieve over the precious time in our lives that was stolen from us. For me, while that time was filled with pain, I feel I also picked up much that was positive, particularly in strengthening my own beliefs. It led me to explore, through my art and writing, both the pleasures we experience and the pain we endure while living in this valley alongside the "real world." It also led me to reexamine the sudden changes in technology and society that took place on the mesa during my childhood— the changes which filled us all, in turn, with both a sense of hope and shock.

I feel the need to reach out to people in the mainstream of society who have no idea what it means to be an Indian, a Navajo, a *Dinéh* child. To those who yearn for vision into our world, I give this collection of paintings, which are pieces of myself.

The book is arranged in a certain order to recreate the essence of my world. Beginning with the spiritual elements and the stories we tell, moving along to memories of my past, then on to members of our community and our rituals, I end on a note of hope with the promise of early spring. Still, you may notice throughout this collection, the constant struggle for balance—balance in living between the "New World" and the ancient world of my people, the Navajo. And ever present, there are the voices of my elders—warning us to guard and protect our mother, the earth.

These are my personal visions and memories of voices shared. A view from within one Navajo family in the midst of changes. Changes from within and without.

Klethla Valley, at the foot of the Shonto plateau in the northern portion of the Navajo Indian Reservation, is the cradle of my youth, and still my home. This is the area that gave birth to the first stirrings of my creative impulses. This is the land that forged my spirit with pain and joy. These are the bittersweet memories that weave their way throughout my canvases.

The philosophy I grew up with taught me to regard all things as having a purpose, as having a spirit—and to treat them accordingly. All things are connected in the great cycle, and nothing can be independent of any part of it. Everything in nature is related. We are all but a small part in this great collection.

The teachings of my elders make it very clear that this land is sacred and that *we* belong to *it*. To desecrate this place in any manner is not acceptable.

I live in a dual society like many in my generation of Navajo. We extract from the past to maintain harmony within. We acknowledge the present and the high-tech world we have been thrust into.

I maintain a square-cornered house in the town of Kayenta, thirty miles from my hogan. In my house, I am involved and connected with the modern world and its conveniences. The telephone, cable television, and fax machine are the trappings in my life now.

The striking differences are played out each weekend when we go back to my hogan, which I built on the site of my birthplace. There, I continue to pray and take part in ceremonies of old. I nurture the stories and lifelines of my elders. I travel in a holy cycle within this round structure. We speak no English there. There is no running water, no television, or telephone. The sun supplies all of our energy. We are in the open, on the mesa, from where you can see far into the distance.

Here, for me, and for you, too, visions and voices from across the mesa—past and present—are recaptured for all time.

—SHONTO BEGAY

ECHOES

▽   ▽   ▽

The songs we sing, the prayers we chant
far into the night,
the sounds of healings and blessings
flowing from the lips of medicine men and women —
these are echoes of the ancient spirits,
that are woven into our stories.

When beings from the Third World
first arrived into the Fourth World,
magic and mystery came with them.
Cicada, Grasshopper, Coyote, Turkey, all their kin
brought with them great power.

The songs we sing, the prayers we chant —
these were the first sounds in the first hogan
upon the new world.
Though different voices from different times —
the songs and chants are the same.
Their magic and power still hang in the air like fog.

First Man and First Woman
appeared upon the Fourth World.
Life was given to them through these songs.
Blessings were given to them through these chants.

They were instructed to rule wisely
and to protect and respect
all that call the earth "Mother."

CREATION

▽　▽　▽

Many winter nights,
my father sat up and told us stories—
stories that came alive through voice and gesture.
Shadows from an old oil drum stove
danced on the hogan wall.
The stove pipe rattled every once in a while
as the snow and wind whined outside.
Tiny drifts of snow sifted through
the cracks in the door.
The story hogan was warm,
the storytelling voice soothing.
He told us stories of creation, of the journey
through four worlds to get to the present one.

First World was the dark world.
Insects lived in the cold.
Unhappiness drove them into the Second World,
the blue world. Birds lived there.
Jealousy ruled and the beings
of the Second World emerged into the Third.
The Third World was inhabited
by larger mammal beings,
Bear, Deer, Coyote, and Wolf,
and all of their cousins.
Life was good in the Third World for many years,
until slowly these beings began to argue
and fight among themselves.
Coyote stole Water-Being's baby
and the Third World was flooded.
The beings moved up to the Fourth World
through a reed.
Locust came up first. Turkey came up last.

First Man and First Woman were created
on the rim of the Fourth World.

The hero twins, Born-for-Water and Monster Slayer,
were born of their mother, Changing Woman,
and their father, the sun.
They were born for a purpose.
Monsters of great size and power roamed the land,
making life miserable for the first people.
The hero twins were to save the people
and the land from these monsters.

In a great battle, mountain ranges fell,
lakes dried up, and the earth trembled.
One by one, the great giants were felled.
These scars and places where Monster fell can still
be seen as mountains, volcanic plugs, and gorges.
After the people of the Fourth World were saved,
they were instructed to rule wisely.
They were placed in charge of maintaining harmony.

They were given the four sacred mountains
as guardians of our holy land, *Diné tah*.

The younger ones are usually asleep by now.
My father ends his story for the night.
There will be many more nights
this winter for stories. The fire in the stove roars,
and shadows on the wall continue their dance.

11

MOTHER'S LACE

▽　▽　▽

In the morning when I leave my hogan,
the mesa echoes with cries of birds.
The air is crisp and clean.
It flows through me, washing away
all ills in my spirit.

Down past the dry wash and slickrock,
across an old wagontrail to my holy ground.
This is the season when the mother
wears lace of ice.

As the sun blazes up from the mesa top,
I sprinkle my corn pollen,
tracing the path of the sun,
as prayer silently leaves my lips.
Prayer of humility, prayer of another day.
Prayer for family, for animals, for travelers.
Prayer especially for *hózhó*, for harmony.
My prayer is strong today.

Far above, a young black hawk spirals,
rising with the fog.
My head is clear, my vision bright;
happiness and love dwell in my heart —
this day starts as all days must,
blessed with prayer:

> *Beauty before me I walk*
> *Beauty behind me I walk*
> *Beauty above me I walk*
> *Beauty below me I walk*
> *Beauty all about me I walk*
> *In beauty all is made whole*
> *In beauty all is restored.*

GRANDMOTHER

▽ ▽ ▽

Grandmother was strong, like a distant mesa.
From her sprang many stories of days long ago.
From her gentle manners
lessons were learned
not easily forgotten.
She told us time and again
that the earth is our mother,
our holy mother.

"Always greet the coming day
by greeting your grandparents,
Yá' át' ééh Shi cheii (Hello, My Grandfather)
to the young juniper tree.
Yá' át' ééh Shi másání (Hello, My Grandmother)
to the young piñon tree."

The lines in her face were marks of honor,
countless winters gazing into the blizzard,
many summers in the hot cornfield.
Her strong brown hands, once smooth,
carried many generations,
gestured many stories,
wiped away many tears.
The whiteness of her windblown hair,
a halo against the setting sun.

My grandmother was called Asdzán Ałts'íísí,
Small Woman. Wife of Little Hat,
mother of generations of Bitter Water Clan,
she lived 113 years.

REFLECTIONS AFTER THE RAIN
▽   ▽   ▽

Little tadpoles dart around my feet
as I stand ankle deep in water
after a brief, but hard summer rainstorm.
The earth smells fresh and delicious.
Fragrance of wet sand always washes away worries.
Distant drifting clouds reflect in the pond
like friendly puffy giants spreading happiness.
In the distance, goat bells tinkle,
letting us know they are near.
My mother sits with her feet in the water,
in silent thoughts of thankfulness.
The water holes are full once again.
We do not have to take the flock
a half day's walk up to the windmill.
Tadpoles tickle my ankles, and I laugh.
On days of no rain my mother tells me stories
as we walk the herd up the mesa,
stories of the land and stories of her childhood.
They are always welcome.
The dogs bark and bells rattle loudly.
Something has startled the flock.
High above against the breaking clouds
a solitary raven appears.
It is time to move the sheep and
the goats back toward home.
I squish my toes into the soft muddy
bottom of the pond, and the tadpoles scatter.
The earth smells delicious.
We are thankful for the rain.

DARKNESS AT NOON
Solar Eclipse

▽   ▽   ▽

I was ten years old when the stars came out at noon. After penning the sheep and goats in the corral for their noon rest, I felt a strange sense of uneasiness. The chirping of birds was absent, the buzzing of insects stopped, even the breeze died down.

My toes felt the sand still warm through the holes in my sneakers. The landscape fell under a shadow on this cloudless day. As I hurried through the tumbleweed and rabbitbrush, it got darker. I looked up and saw twinkling stars far above. The dogs were lying in the doorway.

I ran into the darkened hogan. Immediately I was told to sit down and remain quiet. I couldn't even eat or drink. My aunt said the sun had died. *The sun had died.* The words hit me like thunder. How could this happen? What did we do? I had only started to live. My brothers sat nearby, silent in their own turmoil. The hogan was dark. Only occasional whispers broke the silence.

Outside toward the east, up on the hill, I heard the rising and falling of prayer song. My father was up there boldly standing in the face of darkness, calling back the sun. I prayed silently with him.

As we sat in the darkness for what seemed like eternity, little crescents of light began to appear on the hogan floor, faint at first, then brighter. The sun was returning. It was coming back to life. I prayed harder as the stars disappeared and faint blue washed over the sky. The crescents of light on the floor, coming in from the smokehole, started to round themselves out, becoming half circles, then slowly one full, bright whole. The sun had regained its form. The holy cycle. The sacred symbol of all creation was reborn this day for me.

My father came down from the hill exhausted and happy. We ran out to meet him before the elders could contain us.

That day and all the days since, I appreciate even more the sun we thought we'd lost. The colors are richer and the warmth of the sun, more comforting. The days are brighter. The summer heat is welcome.

Each day, I rise just before the sun does, to sprinkle my corn pollen, and to thank the coming day for its gift of light.

IN MY MOTHER'S KITCHEN

▽ ▽ ▽

Fragrance of fresh tortillas and corn stew
Fills my mother's kitchen
Sparsely furnished
Crowded with warmth
Soot-grayed walls, secretive and blank
She moves gently in and out of light
Like a dream just out of reach

The morning light gives her a halo
That plays upon her crown of dark hair
Strong brown hands caress soft mounds of dough
She gazes out into the warming day
Past sagebrush hills, out towards the foot of Black Mesa
How far would she let the goats wander today
Before it rains

Childhood dreams and warmth
Tight in my throat, tears in my eyes
The radio softly tuned to a local AM station
News of ceremonies and chapter meetings
And funerals
Flows into the peaceful kitchen
Lines upon her face, features carved of hard times
Lines around her eyes, creases of happy times
Bittersweet tears and ringing silvery laughter
I ache in my heart

My mother's gentle movements light up dark corners
Her gentle smiles recall childhood dreams still so alive
My mother moves in and out of light
Like clouds on days of promising rain

MANY FACES, MANY STORIES
▽　▽　▽

Throngs of people crowd the parking lot
Aroma of mutton stew and fried bread
Mingles with the fragrance
　　of cotton candy and popcorn
Today the tribal fair begins

Sounds of traditional song and dance contests
Contrast with blaring bass rap songs
Children cry as mothers and fathers
　　comfort them
Laughter and shouting from the carnival
Sounds of a far-off rodeo announcer
Navajo language mixes with teen language
Cups of coffee and sodas

Many faces, many stories
Many years squinting into the sun
　　looking for lost sheep
Many nights singing at local ceremonies
Many faces that saw the babies' first laugh
Then saw children leaving home
　　to far-off boarding schools
These are the faces of strength
These are the faces of wisdom
These are the faces of many more generations
Of many more tribal fairs

SECOND NIGHT

▽　▽　▽

Voices rise and fall
As they sing into the starry night sky
Faces lit by bonfires, handsome and bold
Like timeless songs we sing tonight.

Second Night of a healing ceremony
One of three nights —
Someone is being restored tonight.

Silhouetted against the fire
Swaying dark bodies
Stepping to the drum's beat
Turquoise and silver flash in the light
Laughter of men, giggles of children
And a nearby grind of a truck engine
Are the sounds
Of this Second Night.

Games of cards off to the side
Movements at the edge of the light
Chasing, tasting
Second Night of healing
Beautiful songs, beautiful voices
Hearts full of prayer
Singers singing deep and strong
Dancers dancing with pride
Second Night of healing ceremony
Someone is restored tonight —
In beauty all is restored.

NIGHT HOLDS MYSTERIES

▽   ▽   ▽

Night holds mysteries
Like day holds light
Wind and movement against the full moon
Bend my courage

Padding on the earthen roof
Sand sifts upon the floor
Barking ends in painful yelps
In the gleam of the bright night
Mystery moves

Youth fragile in fright
Huddle under blankets
Boldness of the day
Gone with the light
Some say I'm fighting night's comfort
Some say night mimics day
Nothing bad
Nothing secret

I say night holds mysteries like day holds light
Sounds still expected, movement now still
It threatens my hearth

Sounds pounding from within
Threaten my spirit
More than the sounds upon the earthen roof

DEATH HOGAN

▽   ▽   ▽

It sits alone and bare in the canyon near here
Someone died inside years ago
The spirit still holds on to the rotted timbers
    and moldy earth

I come upon it now and then
In winter fog, in dust storms
    I don't go near it

It sits cold and stares back
    through darkened holes of weakening logs

Death hogan sits alone and bare in a canyon near here
Someone long ago lived, loved, and laughed here
    Now a spirit dwells silently here
    Alone in a cold, bare canyon

LIFELINE

▽   ▽   ▽

Into the distance we ride
    Upon this road, gray and oily we ride
Toward the sacred mountain of the west
    Toward stories and songs of all-night ceremony
The roar of the wind in our ears
    The smell of fresh oil and sage clings to us.

We have seen ourselves on this road since childhood
    We have sat up front, we have sat in the back
We have felt the dry heat burning our lungs
    We have felt the chill of winter stinging our faces
We have laughed and we have cried upon this road
    We have left more than tire marks upon this road.

This is the lifeline of our land
This road which we travel day and night
This road that connects our communities,
Our families and our responsibilities.
Years from now — into the setting sun,
On this road we will still ride.

DOWN HIGHWAY 163

▽   ▽   ▽

The old lady in the back of the truck
Has seen days much colder
Someone's grandmother
On the highway towards Kayenta
Only her face shows from a faded blanket
Her features are strong
Maybe she is related to the people in the front
Laughing and warm
Or maybe she is catching a ride to the trading post
She may even be returning
From the health clinic in Monument Valley
The back of the truck is cold
Among old spare tires and chains
Shovels and bare metal box
She is no stranger to Old Man Winter
She has seen many winters
It has been colder

NAVAJO POWER PLANT

▽ ▽ ▽

The earth gently releases its roots.
She accepts the gifts of tobacco and corn pollen.

Medicine is plenty upon this plateau.
Reverence is strong, prayers are heard.

Plants to concoct medicine brew, plants to burn for cleansing,
still some to offer in healing to the gods.

My uncle's lips move slightly as silent prayers are passed,
thick brown hands gently placed upon the petals,
arthritic fingers dust the roots.

Carpet of lavender on the vermillion ground
staggers far into the distance between light and shadow.

Concrete fingers stab at the dark summer sky.
Man-made steam clouds rise, white and fragile
against precious black thunderclouds.

Navajo power plant and the powerful healing plant,
they share the same plateau.
One gives us strength and wisdom here and now —
one gives power to strangers somewhere over the horizon —

STORM PATTERN

▽　▽　▽

As a young boy, I sat at my mother's loom.

As she wove, we sang many songs and shared many stories.

Some days

I told her of strange new images

I had seen in magazines,

catalogues and product wrappings.

I tried in vain

to talk her into weaving these

new designs. She would smile and tell me she could not.

She would say

her pattern,

the Tonalea Storm Pattern,

was a gift given to her as a young girl.

A gift of a vision from Spider Woman,

a sacred being of mythic times.

She would say her designs were tributes to storm clouds.

They quivered with life and energy.

My mother still weaves fine rugs.

Variations of her storm pattern. Designs flow easily from her fingertips,

designs she coaxes gently

with songs

from deep within.

I laugh now knowing the new images

I tried so hard to interest her in were corporate logos.

I sat for many years at the foot of her loom,

sharing news from magazines and stories from books

she could not read.

Those days of soft thumping of weaving fork and

heddle, voices low, exchanging, sharing, are still with me.

They are woven into my very being.

Corporate logos,

and the bold, sharp-edged storm pattern against a gray sky.

COYOTE CROSSING

▽ ▽ ▽

"Look up ahead! Old Man Coyote is crossing our path!" My uncle startled my aunt as she swerved slightly, trying to guide the noisy 1976 Ford truck into the glaring evening sun.

"I see him!" my aunt said, pointing into the dirty, insect-splotched windshield that displayed a road map of cracks.

A gray doglike figure slinked across the road up ahead. It tipped its head toward the truck once as ominous tumbleweeds raced past it into the blinding sandstorm.

My aunt slowed down and pulled off onto the shoulder of the road somewhere between Tonalea and Cowsprings.

"I think I have my corn pollen pouch in the glove box!" she said. My uncle rifled through

documents and coupons. They never were sure what all those pieces of paper were for anyway.

He found his wife's pollen pouch finally when all the papers were on the floor. It was stuck in the corner, behind the *Book of Mormon*. Getting out, he groaned like the old door because of the acute angle of the shoulder. He went about thirty feet beyond the truck to where Coyote was last seen.

He stopped and sprinkled corn pollen, first tracing Coyote's path, then tracing the path of the sun in the sky. All along, he uttered a strong prayer:

> *"Mother Earth, Father Sun,*
> *Brothers and Sisters, the beings*
> *   of the earth,*
> *The sky and all those in between*
> *Let me allow the crossing to be a good one.*
> *Bless our old truck and keep us*
> *   out of harm's way.*
> *Mother Earth, Father Sun,*
> *Let his journey be productive as ours will be*
> *Let his journey be safe as ours will be*
> *In beauty all is restored to harmony*
> *In beauty all is restored to harmony*
> *With beauty all around, all is restored."*

He slowly climbed back into the truck as my aunt whined the complaining engine to life.

A respectful silence. They slowly turned and looked into the bed of the truck. They looked at each other and smiled. The European hitchhiker they had picked up just outside of Shonto was quietly sitting back there, nibbling on his organic snack, oblivious to what had just happened.

"Coyote crossing allows us time to reflect upon our journeys," my uncle told me once. "It breaks us free from rushing and taking each other for granted. It is neither a good nor bad omen. It is just how you react to it. Coyote learned all our lessons in mythic times. He carries with him wisdom and strength as well as the dark sides of us. So, here, My Nephew, I give you this pollen bag. Use it often."

OUR MYSTERIES, HIS KNOWLEDGE

▽ ▽ ▽

That which we can only guess to be
    Like voiceless vacant villages of old
    Coyote, Ma'ii, was always there to see
    What the rest of us are only told.

Like pictographs, like broken pottery shards
    We have yet to see this picture whole
    A timeless creature keeping constant guard
    Of what he's seen while playing his many roles.

He's seen diaspora centuries before
    His fur forever ruffled, his senses wide awake
    While watching life and death from his vermillion ledge
    Since the great wind, since the quake.

When Anasazi villages were cleared
    Before his eyes like secrets carved in stone
    He heard silence fall on mesas far and near
    Now the mysteries of our lives are his alone.

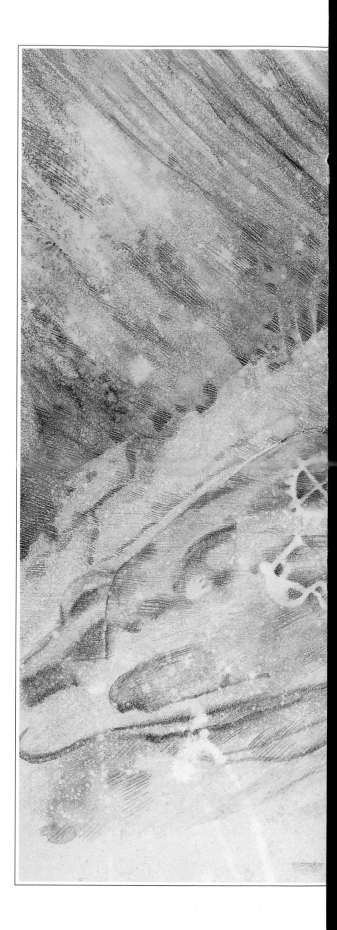

ANASAZI DIASPORA

▽ ▽ ▽

"Shi cheii, My Grandfather, where did the Anasazi people go?"

"Shi' tsoi, My Grandson, the Anasazi had to leave this land long before *Dinéh*, the Navajo people, came into the Fourth World."

"But Grandfather, their villages are still here. Please tell me the story of the people who disappeared."

"Yes, My Grandson, these ancient ones were blessed in many ways. They were taught by the spirits ways to live productive and holy lives. They lived and enjoyed the blessings. They built great cities, they made beautiful pottery, they had fields of golden corn. They needed nothing beyond that. But they became lazy. This offended the spirits."

"How?"

"They chose to live easy lives instead of living by the rules they were taught to maintain holiness."

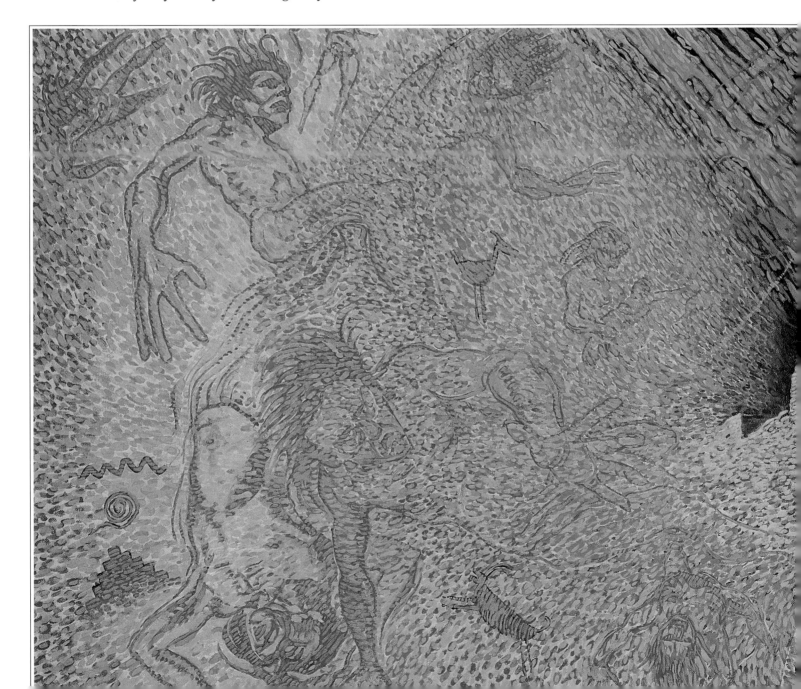

"What were those rules?"

"They were to recognize the gods. To pay them homage. To observe ceremonies. To celebrate seasons. To celebrate births and other stages of life. Special healers were appointed and given power to remove illnesses and restore harmony. But the healers decided to perform this ceremony for everyone, regardless of their health and age. Four times they were warned not to abuse the ceremony. Four times, they chose not to listen."

"And…?"

"On the fifth day, the great wind rose out of the canyon walls and roared throughout the land. People were lifted out of their houses, out of their villages, out of the canyons and valleys. They were scattered throughout this land never to come together again. The buildings were left standing to remind us for all time what will happen if we choose to forget our history, our stories, and above all, our relation to our mother, the earth."

INTO THE NEW WORLD

▽   ▽   ▽

My grandfather's prayer is disturbed
In the morning he walks slowly out the door
Sadness upon his once strong face
With a slow gait, he walks toward the east
The blazing sun rises behind the coal mine upon the mesa
The air smells of smoke not from cookfires
The trampled ground littered with bottles and papers
Souvenirs of ceremony two nights before

My grandfather's prayer is disturbed
The wind that carries his pollen lightly hangs heavy
Trucks on the distant highway blare their impatience
Boughs on piñons and junipers are parched brown
The rain clouds have abandoned us this summer
The watering holes have dried up
Up on the mesa, machines big as buildings
Machines like he's never seen
Continue to rip into the earth

My grandfather's prayer is disturbed
The early sky is already slashed with jet streams
Threads of white from which no water falls
Lightning flash of light from the jet far above
Mocks the thirsty earth
The roar follows far behind, laws of nature distorted

My grandfather's prayer is disturbed
The ground rumbles slightly as the coal train
Takes away another load
Explosives shake the mesa as new veins are opened
The mesa will be smaller this evening

My prayers are disturbed
Still we sprinkle pollen for another day
Still we have faith

EARLY SPRING

▽   ▽   ▽

In the early spring, the snowfall is light
upon the mesa.
It does not stick to the ground very long.
I walk through this patchwork of snow and earth,
watching the ground for early signs.
Signs of growth. Signs of rebirth.

Larkspur and wild onions are still
within the warmth of the earth.
I hear cries of crows off in the distance.
A rabbit bounds off into the sagebrush flat.
A shadow of a hawk disturbs the landscape momentarily.
It sees food and life abundant below that I cannot see.
The cycle of life continues.

Even as I stand here shivering in the afternoon chill,
just below me, young seedlings start
their upward journey.
Insects begin to stir.
Rodents and snakes are comfortable in their burrows.
Maybe to them we also disappear with the cold.
Not to be seen until spring.

For this generation, and many more to come,
this land is beautiful and filled with mysteries.
They reveal themselves and their stories —
if you look very carefully, and listen....

INDEX OF PAINTINGS

▽   ▽   ▽

Story Rock   Acrylic on canvas   42″ x 72″   . . . . Frontispiece

Our Chants, Their Songs (Echoes)   Acrylic on canvas   48″ x 32″   8

Winter Stories (Creation)   Mixed media: watercolor, colored pencil, and ink   20″ x 28″   11

Blessing of My Birthplace (Mother's Lace)   Acrylic on canvas   52″ x 48″   12

In the Late Light (Grandmother)   Acrylic on canvas   38″ x 52″   15

Grandmother Solitude (Reflections After the Rain)   Acrylic on canvas   48″ x 48″   16

Jo'hoona'aii Daz'tsa'   July 1966   (Darkness at Noon: *Solar Eclipse*)   Acrylic on canvas   46″ x 38″   19

In My Mother's Kitchen (In My Mother's Kitchen)   Acrylic on canvas   46″ x 38″   20

The Gathering (Many Faces, Many Stories)   Acrylic on canvas   40″ x 40″   22

Second Night (Second Night)   Acrylic on canvas   48″ x 74″   24

Sent Forth by Night (Night Holds Mysteries)   Acrylic on canvas   48″ x 72″   27

Abandoned (Death Hogan)   Acrylic on canvas   36″ x 44″   29

Brand-new Used on the Promise Road (Lifeline)   Acrylic on canvas   48″ x 76″   30

It Has Been Colder (Down Highway 163)   Acrylic on canvas   42″ x 33½″   32

Navajo Power Plant (Navajo Power Plant)   Acrylic on canvas   36″ x 30″   35

Storm Pattern (Storm Pattern)   Watercolor and pencil on paper   36″ x 24″   36

Coyote Crossing (Coyote Crossing)   Acrylic on canvas   30″ x 40″   38

Our Mysteries, His Knowledge (Our Mysteries, His Knowledge)   Watercolor and pencil on paper   20″ x 28″   . 41

Southwest Diaspora (Anasazi Diaspora)   Acrylic on canvas   24″ x 36″   42

Into the New World (Into the New World)   Acrylic on canvas   36″ x 24″   44

Hunters' Thaw (Early Spring)   Acrylic on canvas   48″ x 48″   47